Insure Your Empire: The Landlord's Ultimate Guide to Rental Property Protection

Jimmy Goodwin

Message from the author

Dear readers,

I'm thrilled that you've chosen my book as your guide to protecting your landlord business. As the branch owner of TWFG Insurance Services in LaGrange, Georgia, I extend a warm and personal invitation to all of you.

If you have any questions or need guidance related to safeguarding your landlord business, I'm here to help. Whether you're a client or not, my goal is to assist you in understanding the complexities of insurance and finding the right solutions for your unique needs.

Feel free to reach out to me directly at jgoodwin@twfg.com. Your success is my priority, and I'm dedicated to providing expert advice and personalized insurance recommendations.

Best regards,

Jimmy Goodwin

Branch Owner, TWFG Insurance Services

www.twfggeorgia.com

LaGrange, GA

Foreword

Dear Readers,

I am delighted to introduce "Insure Your Empire: The Landlord's Ultimate Guide to Rental Property Protection." As the founder of TWFG Insurance Services, LaGrange Ga Branch and a seasoned insurance expert specializing in commercial and select personal insurance clients, I understand the critical importance of safeguarding your rental properties.

This comprehensive eBook has been meticulously crafted to provide rental property owners like you with actionable insights, valuable tips, and expert advice on navigating the complex world of insurance. Whether you are a seasoned landlord or just starting your real estate journey, this handbook will equip you with the knowledge and tools to protect your investments and secure your financial future.

Through the chapters of this eBook, you will explore the different types of insurance coverage, understand how to select the right policies for your rental properties and learn about loss of rental income coverage to mitigate financial setbacks. Additionally, you will delve into the power of umbrella insurance, the claims process, and the significance of policy exclusions.

I encourage you to read this eBook with an open mind and a desire to protect your rental empire proactively. Remember, insurance is more than just a safety net; it is the shield that guards your hard work, dedication, and vision for a prosperous future.

Wishing you success and prosperity in your journey to safeguarding your rentals!

Sincerely,

Jimmy Goodwin

Branch Owner, TWFG Insurance Services

Disclaimer:

"Insure Your Empire: The Landlord's Ultimate Guide to Rental Property Protection" is intended for informational purposes only. The content provided in this book is not intended as professional insurance advice or legal counsel.

While the information presented in this book is based on general insurance principles and practices at the time of publication, insurance policies and regulations may vary based on geographic locations, insurance carriers, and individual circumstances. Therefore, the information may not be applicable to all situations or jurisdictions.

Although efforts have been made to ensure the accuracy and relevance of the information provided, the authors and publishers of this book are not responsible for any errors or omissions that may occur. The authors and publishers disclaim any liability for actions taken or not taken based on the content of this eBook.

Insurance coverage and requirements are subject to change over time. Therefore, readers are encouraged to verify the information with their insurance agents or relevant authorities for the most up-to-date and accurate advice.

The book may contain references to external websites or resources for informational purposes. However, the authors and publishers do not endorse or have control over the content, accuracy, or availability of those external resources.

By accessing and using this book, readers agree to hold harmless the authors, publishers, and contributors from any liabilities or claims arising from the use of the information provided herein.

It is essential for readers to exercise their due diligence and judgment when applying the concepts and recommendations in this book to their individual circumstances. Your insurance coverage decisions should be based on comprehensive evaluations and discussions with qualified professionals.

Please note that this book does not serve as an insurance policy or insurance contract. Actual insurance coverage will be governed solely by the terms and conditions of the insurance policy and relevant legal regulations in place at the time of purchase.

By continuing to read and utilize this book, readers acknowledge and accept the terms of this disclaimer. If you do not agree with any part of this disclaimer, we kindly request that you refrain from accessing or using the book.

Table of Contents

Copyright Notice
  - © 2023 Jimmy Goodwin

Chapter 1: Insurance Essentials for Landlords

1.1 Types of Insurance Coverage for Rental Properties

As a landlord, one of the most crucial decisions is choosing the right insurance coverage for your rental properties. Understanding the different types of insurance available is essential to protect your investments and manage potential risks effectively.

a) Property Insurance: This foundational coverage protects your rental property's structure from various perils, including fire, vandalism, and certain natural disasters. It typically covers the building itself and any fixtures, such as built-in appliances, flooring, and countertops. Property insurance is a fundamental policy every landlord should have to safeguard their real estate investments.

b) Liability Insurance: Liability coverage is equally vital, as it protects you from potential lawsuits related to injuries or property damage that may occur on your rental property. Suppose a tenant or visitor gets injured on your property and holds you responsible. In that case, liability insurance can cover legal expenses, medical bills, and other costs that might arise from the lawsuit. Without liability coverage, you could be at risk of significant financial losses.

c) Loss of Rental Income Coverage: This insurance protects landlords from income loss caused by covered perils that render a rental property uninhabitable. If your property becomes unlivable due to a covered event, such as a fire or severe storm, loss of rental income coverage can help you recover the rental income you would have earned during the repair period. This can be a lifeline during unforeseen disruptions and ensure you continue to receive income despite the property's temporary unavailability.

1.2 Assessing Your Insurance Needs as a Landlord

Determining the suitable insurance needs for your rental properties requires a thoughtful and thorough evaluation of various factors. Take the following into consideration when assessing your insurance needs:

a) Property Value and Replacement Cost: Determine the replacement cost of your rental property, which is the amount needed to rebuild the property in the event of a total loss. This value differs from the property's market value and should be used to determine the appropriate coverage level.

b) Location and Risks: Consider the location of your rental property and the associated risks. Properties in areas prone to natural disasters or higher crime rates may require additional coverage.

c) Number of Properties: If you own multiple rental properties, you may be eligible for a multi-property discount by insuring them under a single policy or with the same insurance provider. This can lead to cost savings and simplified management.

d) Type of Rental Property: Your property type can influence the coverage needed. For instance, a commercial property may require specific endorsements that a residential property doesn't need.

1.3 Obtaining Multiple Quotes and Comparing Policies

Once you clearly understand your insurance needs, shopping around for multiple insurance quotes and comparing policies is essential. Don't settle for the first policy that comes your way; instead, consider the following steps to ensure you get the best coverage at the most competitive price:

a) Reach Out to Insurance Providers: Contact different insurance companies or agents specializing in landlord insurance to request quotes tailored to your specific needs. Provide accurate information to receive accurate quotes.

b) Compare Coverage and Deductibles: Review each policy's coverage limits, exclusions, and deductibles. Consider the level of protection each policy offers and how much you would need to pay out of pocket before coverage kicks in (the deductible).

c) Evaluate Additional Endorsements: Some insurance providers offer optional endorsements to enhance coverage. Evaluate these options carefully to see if they align with your needs and budget.

d) Check Customer Reviews: Look up customer reviews and ratings for the insurance providers you are considering. Positive reviews and feedback can indicate a reliable and responsive insurer.

By investing time and effort in this process, you can find the insurance policy that provides comprehensive coverage at a reasonable cost, ensuring your rental properties are well-protected for years.

Chapter 2: Selecting the Right Coverage for Your Properties

When it comes to insuring your rental properties, it's crucial to choose the appropriate insurance coverage that aligns with your role as a landlord. As you venture into the world of rental property management, understanding the distinctions between commercial and personal insurance will empower you to make an informed decision based on your unique circumstances and property portfolio.

2.1 Commercial Insurance for Business Entities:

Commercial insurance is specifically designed for properties owned by business entities, such as corporations, limited liability companies (LLCs), or partnerships. If you are a business entity and own commercial rental properties, including office buildings, retail spaces, warehouses, and apartment buildings, consider the following key aspects of commercial insurance:

- Commercial Dwellings Coverage: For business entities that own residential rental properties such as apartment buildings, commercial dwelling policies (e.g., DP-1 or DP-3) are the appropriate choice. These policies provide comprehensive coverage tailored to properties used primarily for business purposes.

- Comprehensive Coverage: Commercial insurance policies offer a broader range of coverage options, addressing the unique risks associated with commercial properties. They typically include coverage for property damage, business interruption, equipment breakdown, and liability arising from business operations.

- Higher Liability Limits: Commercial properties often have higher risks and potential liability. Therefore, commercial insurance policies usually offer higher liability limits to protect business entity landlords from significant lawsuits.

- Flexibility in Endorsements: Business entities can benefit from the flexibility of endorsements, which are add-ons or modifications to standard insurance policies. Endorsements allow you to customize your coverage to meet your specific needs, providing an added layer of protection.

2.2 Personal Insurance for Individual Landlords:

Personal insurance, also known as homeowners insurance, is NOT suitable for properties owned by individuals who act as landlords. If you are an individual landlord and own a limited number of rental properties, such as 1-4 family dwellings, homeowners insurance is NOT the appropriate choice. Instead, consider the following key aspects of insurance coverage suitable for individual landlords:

- Coverage Form DP-1 or DP-3: Individual landlords would typically be covered under personal dwelling policies (e.g., DP-1 or DP-3) designed for rental properties used primarily for residential purposes.

- Limited Business Use Coverage: Personal insurance may provide some limited coverage for rental properties if they are used primarily for residential purposes. However, it may not adequately protect against certain business-related risks that commercial insurance addresses.

- Standard Liability Limits: Personal insurance policies typically offer standard liability limits, which may be sufficient for rental properties with lower risk factors compared to commercial properties.

- Potential Coverage Gaps: It's important to be aware that personal insurance does not fully cover certain business-related risks. As an individual landlord, you may face potential coverage gaps that could leave you vulnerable to financial losses.

2.3 The Power of Customization: Additional Endorsements

Regardless of whether you choose commercial or personal insurance, the power of customization lies in the ability to add endorsements to your insurance policy. These endorsements allow you to tailor your coverage to the specific needs of your rental properties. Consider the following endorsements:

- Water Damage Endorsement: Extends coverage for water damage caused by events like sewer backups, sump pump failures, and water leaks, which can be common and costly issues for rental properties.

- Ordinance or Law Coverage: Helps cover the additional expenses incurred to comply with current building codes if your rental property suffers damage.

- Earthquake or Flood Coverage: Consider adding these endorsements for comprehensive protection if your rental property is located in an area prone to earthquakes or floods.

- Identity Theft Coverage: Include identity theft protection in your insurance policy to receive assistance in the event of identity theft-related expenses.

By carefully selecting the appropriate insurance coverage based on your role as a landlord, tailoring your policy to your unique rental properties, and leveraging endorsements where necessary, you can ensure that your investments are well-protected and that you have peace of mind as you manage your rental property business. Remember, homeowners insurance is never suitable for anyone acting as a landlord, and it's essential to choose the right coverage to safeguard your valuable assets.

Chapter 3: Safeguarding Your Rental Properties

3.1 Property Protection Insurance: A Comprehensive Shield

As a landlord, protecting your rental properties from unforeseen risks is paramount to maintaining a successful and profitable real estate portfolio. Property protection insurance serves as a comprehensive shield that guards your investments against a wide range of perils. Understanding the components of this coverage will help you fortify your rental properties effectively.

a) Coverage for Property Damage: Property protection insurance provides coverage for damages to the structure of your rental property caused by covered perils such as fire, lightning, windstorms, vandalism, and certain natural disasters. This coverage is essential as it ensures your property is repaired or rebuilt in the event of a covered loss, allowing you to quickly restore your investment.

b) Protection for Attached Structures: In addition to covering the main building, property protection insurance may extend to attached structures such as garages, sheds, and fences. Ensuring these structures are adequately covered prevents potential out-of-pocket expenses for repairs or replacements.

c) Coverage for Personal Belongings (Contents Insurance): If your rental property is furnished or includes appliances and other personal belongings, you may opt for contents insurance as part of your property protection coverage. Contents insurance provides reimbursement for damaged or stolen items within the rental property.

3.2 Fire, Theft, and Natural Disasters: Coverage Options

Rental property owners face various risks, ranging from common hazards like fire and theft to the unpredictable forces of nature. Understanding the coverage options for these specific perils can help you choose the right insurance to safeguard your properties.

a) Fire Insurance: Fire insurance is a foundational component of property protection coverage. It provides financial protection in the event of damage caused by fire or smoke. Fires can be devastating, but with proper insurance coverage, you can recover swiftly without incurring significant financial burdens.

b) Theft Insurance: Theft insurance covers losses resulting from burglary or theft of personal property from your rental property. This coverage can help you replace stolen items and secure your property against future incidents.

c) Natural Disaster Coverage: Depending on your rental property's location, you may need additional coverage for specific natural disasters such as hurricanes, earthquakes, or floods. Standard property protection insurance may not include coverage for these events, making additional endorsements or separate policies necessary.

3.3 Proactive Measures: Implementing Safety and Security

While insurance coverage provides vital protection, taking proactive measures to enhance safety and security can further safeguard your rental properties and reduce risks.

a) Installing Security Systems: Consider installing security systems, including burglar alarms, surveillance cameras, and motion sensor lighting. These measures not only deter criminals but can also lead to insurance premium discounts.

b) Conducting Regular Inspections: Regularly inspect your rental properties to identify potential safety hazards or maintenance issues. Promptly addressing problems can prevent them from escalating into more significant concerns.

c) Implementing Safety Measures: Enhance safety within the property by installing smoke detectors, carbon monoxide detectors, and fire extinguishers. Inform tenants about emergency procedures and the location of safety equipment.

d) Enforcing Tenant Screening: Thoroughly screen prospective tenants to ensure they have a history of responsible renting and the financial ability to meet rental obligations. This can reduce the likelihood of property damage or unpaid rent.

By combining robust property protection insurance with proactive safety and security measures, you can build a strong defense against potential risks and ensure the long-term success of your rental property investments. Safeguarding your rental properties benefits not only you as the landlord but also your tenants, as it creates a safe and secure environment for them to call home.

Chapter 4: Loss of Rental Income Coverage

4.1 Understanding Loss of Rental Income Coverage

As a landlord, your rental income is a crucial source of financial stability. However, unforeseen events such as property damage from covered perils can disrupt your rental business and lead to significant income loss. Loss of rental income coverage is a specialized insurance option designed to mitigate the financial impact of such disruptions.

a) Coverage for Income Loss: Loss of rental income coverage provides financial protection when your rental property becomes uninhabitable due to a covered peril, such as a fire or severe storm. If your property requires repairs and cannot generate rental income during the restoration period, this coverage can replace the lost income you would have earned.

b) Reimbursement for Extra Expenses: In addition to replacing lost rental income, this coverage may also reimburse you for reasonable extra expenses incurred while your property is undergoing repairs. These expenses could include temporary accommodations for displaced tenants or the cost of marketing your property to attract new tenants after the repairs are completed.

c) Duration of Coverage: Loss of rental income coverage typically has a specified time limit or maximum coverage period, which may vary depending on your policy. Understanding these limitations will help you plan for the potential duration of income loss.

4.2 Mitigating Financial Setbacks During Repairs

When your rental property is damaged and rendered uninhabitable, the loss of rental income can have severe financial repercussions. Loss of rental income coverage offers a lifeline during these challenging times, helping you stay afloat financially and navigate the repair process more smoothly.

a) Calculating the Income Loss: The first step in utilizing loss of rental income coverage is to calculate the income loss accurately. Your insurance provider will require documentation of your rental income, such as rental agreements and past rental history, to determine the appropriate coverage amount.

b) Filing a Claim: In the event of property damage, contact your insurance provider promptly to file a claim for loss of rental income. Provide all necessary documentation, including proof of the covered peril, repair estimates, and documentation of your rental income.

c) Coordinating Repairs: While your insurance claim is being processed, coordinate with contractors and repair professionals to begin the restoration process as soon as possible. Timely repairs can help minimize the duration of income loss.

d) Keep Detailed Records: Throughout the repair period, keep detailed records of all expenses related to the loss of rental income and extra expenses. This documentation will be crucial when submitting reimbursement claims to your insurance provider.

4.3 Calculating Coverage Limit: Protecting Your Income Stream

When selecting loss of rental income coverage, it's essential to determine an appropriate coverage limit that adequately protects your rental income stream. Consider the following factors when calculating the coverage limit:

a) Rental Income Amount: Calculate your average monthly rental income and multiply it by the estimated number of months your property may remain uninhabitable. This will give you an initial estimate of the coverage limit needed.

b) Restoration Timeframe: Consider the typical time it takes to complete repairs and restoration after a covered peril. Ensure your coverage limit aligns with the potential duration of income loss.

c) Additional Expenses: Account for any extra expenses you may incur, such as advertising costs to attract new tenants or increased mortgage payments during the repair period.

d) Risk Assessment: Evaluate the potential risks your rental property may face, such as the likelihood of certain covered perils in your area. Adjust your coverage limit accordingly to address higher-risk scenarios.

By carefully calculating the coverage limit and securing adequate loss of rental income coverage, you can protect your income stream and maintain financial stability during unexpected property disruptions. This proactive approach to risk management ensures that you can continue to meet your financial obligations and protect your real estate investments even in challenging times.

Chapter 5: The Power of Umbrella Insurance

5.1 An Extra Layer of Protection: What is Umbrella Insurance?

As a landlord, your rental properties are valuable assets that generate income and provide financial security. However, with significant assets also come increased liability risks. To fortify your overall insurance protection and shield your assets from potential lawsuits, consider the power of umbrella insurance.

a) Understanding Umbrella Insurance: Umbrella insurance is a supplementary liability policy that extends beyond the limits of your primary insurance policies, such as property and liability insurance. It acts as an "umbrella" of additional coverage, providing an extra layer of financial protection for your assets and helping safeguard your wealth.

b) Broad Coverage: Umbrella insurance covers a wide range of liability risks, including personal injury claims, property damage liability, and even certain lawsuits not covered by your primary policies. It serves as a safety net, offering increased coverage limits that can protect you against costly legal judgments.

c) Comprehensive Protection: This insurance is not limited to just your rental properties; it can extend to other aspects of your life, such as your personal residence, vehicles, and certain watercraft. This comprehensive protection ensures you are shielded from potential financial devastation that could arise from various liability situations.

5.2 Evaluating Coverage Needs for Added Security

To determine if umbrella insurance is a valuable addition to your insurance portfolio, carefully assess your unique situation and liability risks. Several factors can help you evaluate your coverage needs for added security.

a) Asset Value: Consider the total value of your assets, including your rental properties, personal residence, savings, investments, and other valuable possessions. Umbrella insurance should provide sufficient coverage to protect these assets in the event of a liability claim.

b) Potential Risks: Evaluate your liability risks as a landlord and in other areas of your life. These risks may include property-related accidents, auto accidents, or other situations where you could be held legally responsible for damages.

c) Existing Coverage Limits: Review the liability limits of your primary insurance policies, such as your property and auto insurance. Compare these limits to your total asset value and potential liability risks to identify any gaps that umbrella insurance could fill.

d) Peace of Mind: Beyond financial considerations, umbrella insurance can provide peace of mind. Knowing that you have an added layer of protection against unforeseen and potentially catastrophic events can alleviate stress and worry.

5.3 Commercial Property Coverage and Umbrella Insurance

If you own commercial rental properties, umbrella insurance can play a crucial role in protecting your business and personal assets from significant liability risks.

a) Enhanced Protection for Commercial Properties: Commercial rental properties carry additional liability risks due to their business nature. Umbrella insurance offers increased coverage limits that can protect you from costly lawsuits arising from commercial property-related incidents.

b) Personal and Business Integration: As a landlord, your personal and business lives may intertwine, especially if you own multiple properties or operate as a sole proprietorship. Umbrella insurance can seamlessly integrate both personal and business liability coverage under a single policy.

c) Risk Management: Implementing umbrella insurance as part of your risk management strategy demonstrates your commitment to protecting your rental empire and personal wealth. This proactive approach can help deter potential legal actions and show that you are prepared to handle any liability situation that may arise.

d) Consult with an Insurance Professional: Evaluating your coverage needs and identifying the right umbrella insurance policy can be complex. Consult with an experienced insurance professional who can assess your specific situation and recommend the most appropriate coverage based on your assets and potential risks.

By considering the power of umbrella insurance and integrating it into your overall insurance strategy, you can strengthen your protection as a landlord and safeguard your assets against the uncertainties of liability risks. Umbrella insurance offers peace of mind and an added layer of financial security, allowing you to focus on managing and expanding your rental properties with confidence.

Chapter 6: Navigating Insurance Claims and Policies

6.1 The Claims Process: Your Path to Recovery

Insurance is a critical safety net that provides financial protection in times of need. When unforeseen events such as property damage or liability claims occur, navigating the insurance claims process becomes essential for your path to recovery.

a) Prompt Action: In the event of a covered incident, take prompt action to initiate the claims process. Contact your insurance provider as soon as possible and provide them with all the necessary details regarding the incident.

b) Documentation: Document the damage or incident thoroughly. Take photos or videos of the affected areas and any relevant evidence. Keep records of conversations and communications with tenants, witnesses, and authorities, as these can be valuable during the claims process.

c) File the Claim: Submit a complete and accurate claim form to your insurance provider. Include all required documentation and supporting evidence to support your claim.

d) Adjuster's Visit: Depending on the nature of the claim, an insurance adjuster may visit your rental property to assess the damage or gather information. Cooperate fully and provide the adjuster with access to the necessary areas.

e) Claim Settlement: Once your claim has been evaluated and processed, your insurance provider will determine the appropriate settlement amount based on your policy's coverage and limits. If the claim is approved, you will receive the agreed-upon compensation.

f) Dispute Resolution: If you disagree with the settlement offer or claim denial, work with your insurance provider to resolve any disputes. You may seek the advice of a legal professional if necessary.

6.2 Policy Exclusions: What Isn't Covered

While insurance provides essential protection, it's important to be aware of policy exclusions. Policy exclusions are specific events or circumstances that your insurance policy does not cover. Understanding these exclusions can help you take appropriate measures to address potential gaps in coverage.

a) Review Your Policy: Regularly review your insurance policy to understand its specific exclusions. Pay close attention to sections that outline coverage limitations and scenarios not covered by your policy.

b) Additional Coverage: If you identify gaps in coverage or areas of concern, consult with your insurance provider to explore options for additional coverage or endorsements that address your specific needs.

c) Stay Informed: Keep yourself informed about changes to your policy and updates to coverage. Insurance policies may be updated periodically, so it's essential to stay up-to-date with your coverage.

6.3 Depreciation and Replacement Cost Coverage Explained

When insuring your rental properties, it's crucial to understand how depreciation and replacement cost coverage can impact your claims.

a) Depreciation: Depreciation is the decrease in the value of an asset over time. In the context of insurance claims, depreciation is considered when determining the actual cash value (ACV) of damaged property. ACV is the cost to replace or repair the damaged property minus depreciation.

b) Replacement Cost Coverage: Replacement cost coverage, on the other hand, provides compensation for the full cost of replacing or repairing damaged property without accounting for depreciation. This coverage allows you to replace your property with similar, new items or materials.

c) Consideration for Claims: When filing a claim, the type of coverage you have will impact the reimbursement you receive. If you have replacement cost coverage, you will be compensated for the full cost of replacement or repair, while actual cash value coverage considers depreciation.

d) Importance of Coverage Selection: Selecting the right coverage option can significantly affect your ability to recover from a loss. Replacement cost coverage provides better financial protection and can help you restore your rental property to its pre-loss condition without substantial out-of-pocket expenses.

Navigating insurance claims and understanding policy exclusions can be complex, but it is essential to protect your rental properties effectively. By being proactive and informed, you can confidently manage potential risks, ensuring that your insurance coverage provides the support you need in times of uncertainty. Remember, a well-protected rental empire is not only a testament to your business acumen but also a solid foundation for long-term financial success.

Conclusion

Congratulations! You have completed the journey through "Insure Your Empire: The Landlord's Ultimate Guide to Rental Property Protection." Throughout this comprehensive eBook, we have explored the essential aspects of insurance for landlords, equipping you with the knowledge and tools to safeguard your rental properties and secure your financial future.

In this handbook, we started by understanding the critical importance of insurance for landlords and the various types of coverage available. We delved into the process of assessing your insurance needs and obtaining multiple quotes to find the most suitable policies for your rental properties.

We explored the power of customization through additional endorsements, tailoring your coverage to address unique risks and protect both your property and personal belongings. Understanding property protection insurance helped you recognize the comprehensive shield that guards your investments against perils such as fire, theft, and natural disasters.

We then turned our attention to loss of rental income coverage, a valuable lifeline during unforeseen disruptions that may lead to income loss. By calculating coverage limits and coordinating repairs efficiently, you can mitigate financial setbacks and quickly recover from property damage.

Next, we discovered the advantages of umbrella insurance, which offers an extra layer of protection beyond your primary policies. Evaluating your coverage needs and integrating umbrella insurance into your insurance portfolio can enhance your overall protection and provide peace of mind.

Finally, we explored the intricacies of navigating insurance claims and understanding policy exclusions. By being well-informed about the claims process and policy limitations, you can confidently manage potential challenges and ensure your rental properties remain well-protected.

As you continue your journey as a landlord, remember that insurance is not just a formality but a crucial aspect of securing your investments and mitigating risks. Embrace the proactive approach to risk management, combining insurance coverage with safety measures to fortify your rental empire.

At TWFG Insurance Services, we are committed to helping you make informed insurance decisions. Should you have any further questions or require assistance, our experienced team is here to support you.

Thank you for choosing "Insure Your Empire: The Landlord's Ultimate Guide to Rental Property Protection." May this knowledge empower you to build and safeguard a successful rental business that thrives for years to come.

Wishing you prosperity and continued success in your journey as a landlord.

Sincerely,

Jimmy Goodwin
Branch Owner, TWFG Insurance Services
Lagrange Ga

Glossary of Terms

1. Acts of Terrorism: Deliberate acts of violence, including bombings, hijackings, or other malicious acts, intended to create fear and intimidate a population, usually excluded from standard insurance policies.

2. Adjusters: Professionals employed by insurance companies to assess the extent of damages and losses resulting from covered events.

3. Business Use: Utilizing a rental property for commercial purposes, which may lead to certain damages not being covered by standard insurance policies.

4. Claims Handler: A dedicated professional employed by insurance companies to manage and oversee the entire claims process on behalf of the policyholder.

5. Commercial Property Insurance: Insurance coverage specifically designed to protect the physical structure and contents of commercial rental properties.

6. Deductible: The amount a policyholder must pay out of pocket before the insurance coverage comes into effect for a claim.

7. Depreciation: The reduction in the value of a property or asset over time, which may be factored into claim settlements by insurance companies.

8. Dwelling Coverage: Insurance that protects the structure of a rental property itself against damages from covered perils.

9. Earthquake Coverage: Insurance coverage specifically designed to protect against damages resulting from earthquakes.

10. Exclusions: Scenarios and events not covered by an insurance policy, which policyholders should be aware of to manage expectations.

11. Flood Coverage: Insurance coverage specifically designed to protect against damages resulting from floods.

12. General Liability Coverage: Insurance that provides protection against liability claims for bodily injury or property damage caused to others.

13. Hurricane Preparedness: Taking proactive measures to protect a property from potential damages caused by hurricanes.

14. Intentional Damage: Deliberate harm caused by the landlord or tenants, typically not covered by insurance.

15. Loss of Rental Income Coverage: Insurance coverage that compensates for rental income lost during repairs or restoration of a rental property due to covered perils.

16. Natural Disasters: Catastrophic events caused by natural forces, such as hurricanes, earthquakes, and floods.

17. Personal Property Coverage: Insurance that provides compensation for personal belongings owned by the landlord and present in the rental property.

18. Policy Exclusions: Specific circumstances or events not covered by an insurance policy.

19. Replacement Cost Coverage: Insurance coverage that compensates for the actual cost of replacing or repairing damaged items without considering depreciation.

20. Risk Exposure: The assessment of potential liability risks associated with a rental property.

21. Smoke Alarms: Devices installed in rental properties to detect smoke and provide early warning of potential fires.

22. Terrorism Coverage: Insurance coverage specifically designed to protect against damages resulting from acts of terrorism.

23. Umbrella Insurance: Additional liability insurance that supplements primary insurance policies and offers higher liability limits.

24. Vacant Property Insurance: Insurance coverage designed specifically for unoccupied rental properties for an extended period.

25. Vandalism Coverage: Insurance coverage that provides protection against damages resulting from deliberate destruction of rental property.

26. Wear and Tear: Gradual deterioration of a property over time, typically not covered by insurance.

Frequently Asked Questions (FAQs)

Q1: Why do I need insurance for my rental properties?
A: Insurance for rental properties is essential for protecting your real estate investments from unforeseen risks. It provides financial security in the event of property damage, liability claims, or income loss, ensuring that you can recover and maintain your rental business even during challenging times.

Q2: What types of insurance do I need for my rental properties?
A: As a landlord, you typically need property insurance to protect the physical structure of your rental property from perils like fire, theft, and natural disasters. Liability insurance is also crucial, as it covers potential lawsuits arising from injuries or property damage on your property. Depending on your property type and needs, you may also consider loss of rental income coverage and umbrella insurance for added protection.

Q3: How can I save money on insurance for my rental properties?
A: There are several ways to save money on insurance for your rental properties. First, obtain multiple quotes from different insurance providers to compare coverage and pricing. Consider bundling multiple policies under one insurance provider for potential discounts. Implement safety measures, such as installing security systems, to reduce risks and qualify for insurance premium reductions.

Q4: Do I need umbrella insurance if I already have property and liability insurance?
A: While property and liability insurance provide essential coverage, umbrella insurance offers an additional layer of protection with higher liability limits. It can protect your assets beyond the limits of your primary policies and provide comprehensive coverage for both your rental properties and personal life. If you have substantial assets or face higher liability risks, umbrella insurance can be a valuable addition to your insurance portfolio.

Q5: How do I file an insurance claim for my rental property?

A: If your rental property experiences a covered incident, contact your insurance provider immediately to initiate the claims process. Provide all necessary documentation, including photos or videos of the damage and any supporting evidence. Work with your insurance adjuster to assess the damage, and file a complete claim form with all required information. Keep records of all communications and expenses related to the claim.

Q6: Will my insurance cover tenant-related damages?
A: Property insurance typically covers damages caused by covered perils, regardless of who or what caused the damage. However, it's essential to distinguish between tenant negligence and regular wear and tear. While insurance may cover accidental damages caused by tenants, regular maintenance and minor wear and tear are the landlord's responsibility.

Q7: Can I adjust my insurance coverage as my rental property portfolio grows?
A: Absolutely! As your rental property portfolio evolves, you can adjust your insurance coverage to match your changing needs. Review your insurance policies regularly and consult with your insurance provider to ensure you have adequate coverage for the number and type of properties you own.

Q8: Are there any specific insurance requirements for commercial rental properties?
A: Yes, commercial rental properties may have unique insurance requirements compared to residential properties. Commercial insurance typically provides broader coverage tailored to business-related risks. If you own commercial rental properties, ensure your insurance coverage addresses the specific liabilities and risks associated with these properties.

Q9: Can I transfer my insurance to a new property I acquire?
A: If you purchase a new rental property, you may be able to transfer your existing insurance policy to cover the new property, provided it meets the insurer's underwriting guidelines. However, it's essential to inform your insurance provider about the new property and make any necessary adjustments to your coverage.

Q10: How can I ensure I have sufficient coverage for potential liability claims?
A: To ensure you have sufficient coverage for potential liability claims, review your liability limits regularly. Evaluate your asset value, potential risks, and the likelihood of facing significant lawsuits. If necessary, consider increasing your liability limits or adding umbrella insurance to provide additional protection beyond your primary policies.

Please note that while these FAQs provide general information, your insurance needs and requirements may vary based on your individual circumstances and location. It's crucial to consult with an experienced insurance professional to get personalized advice and tailored coverage for your rental property business.

10 Questions to Ask When Interviewing Your Future Insurance Agent

Choosing the right insurance agent is a critical step in ensuring you receive the best coverage and service for your insurance needs. Before making a decision, take the time to interview potential insurance agents to find the one who aligns with your goals and priorities. Here are ten essential questions to ask during the interview process:

1. What Types of Insurance Do You Specialize In?
   - Understanding the agent's areas of expertise will help you determine if they can cater to your specific insurance needs, such as property insurance, liability insurance, or umbrella coverage.

2. How Many Years of Experience Do You Have as an Insurance Agent?
   - An experienced insurance agent will likely have a deeper understanding of the insurance industry and the ability to offer well-informed advice.

3. Do You Have Experience Working with Landlords or Rental Property Owners?
   - If you are a landlord, it's crucial to work with an agent familiar with the unique insurance requirements and risks associated with rental properties.

4. Which Insurance Companies Do You Represent?
   - Knowing the insurance companies an agent represents will give you insight into the range of policies they can offer and the diversity of coverage options available.

5. How Do You Determine the Ideal Coverage for Your Clients?
   - A good insurance agent should take the time to understand your individual needs and risk profile before recommending suitable coverage options.

6. Can You Provide References or Testimonials from Satisfied Clients?

  - Requesting references or testimonials can give you an idea of the agent's reputation and the level of satisfaction their clients have experienced.

7. What Is Your Approach to Handling Insurance Claims?
  - Inquire about the agent's process for handling insurance claims to ensure they can efficiently assist you during challenging times.

8. How Do You Stay Updated on Changes in the Insurance Industry?
  - An agent who stays informed about industry trends and policy updates is more likely to provide you with relevant and up-to-date coverage options.

9. Do You Offer Customized Coverage Plans or Additional Endorsements?
  - Customized coverage plans and additional endorsements can tailor your insurance policy to your specific needs and provide comprehensive protection.

10. How Will You Ensure My Insurance Needs Are Met as My Rental Property Portfolio Grows?
  - As your rental property portfolio expands, you'll need an agent who can adapt your insurance coverage to match your changing needs.

Remember to take notes during each interview and compare the answers to make an informed decision. Choose an insurance agent who not only provides the right coverage but also demonstrates a commitment to outstanding customer service and a genuine interest in protecting your assets.

Disclaimer: These questions are intended as a guide and may be adjusted based on your unique insurance requirements and preferences. Always consult with the insurance agent directly to get personalized advice and information.

Understanding Co-Insurance and the Co-Insurance Penalty
Formula

What is Co-Insurance?

Co-insurance is a common provision found in property insurance
policies, designed to encourage policyholders to adequately
insure their properties. It requires the policyholder to maintain
insurance coverage that is equal to or above a specified
percentage of the property's value, typically 80% or 90%. This
percentage represents the co-insurance requirement.

The purpose of co-insurance is to ensure that policyholders
carry an appropriate level of insurance coverage relative to the
value of their property. By doing so, insurance companies can
more accurately assess risks and establish fair premiums.

How Does Co-Insurance Work?

When a property owner carries insurance coverage below the
co-insurance requirement, they are considered underinsured. In
the event of a partial loss, the insurance company will apply a
co-insurance penalty to the claim settlement.

The co-insurance penalty is calculated based on the proportion
of coverage the policyholder carried compared to the required
amount. The penalty results in the policyholder assuming a
larger portion of the loss than they would if they were
adequately insured.

The Co-Insurance Penalty Formula

The co-insurance penalty formula is straightforward and is used
to calculate the financial consequences of being underinsured. It
is as follows:

Co-Insurance Penalty = (Actual Insurance Coverage / Required
Insurance Coverage) x Total Loss

Example Scenario

Let's consider a property with a total value of $500,000, and the insurance policy has an 80% co-insurance requirement, meaning the required insurance coverage is $400,000 (80% of $500,000).

If the policyholder only carries $300,000 in insurance coverage at the time of a partial loss, the co-insurance penalty would be calculated as follows:

Co-Insurance Penalty = ($300,000 / $400,000) x Total Loss

Suppose the total loss amount is $100,000. In that case, the co-insurance penalty would be:

Co-Insurance Penalty = (0.75) x $100,000 = $75,000

In this scenario, the policyholder's underinsured amount of $100,000 resulted in a co-insurance penalty of $75,000. As a result, they would be responsible for a larger portion of the loss, while the insurance company would only cover the remaining portion.

Importance of Meeting Co-Insurance Requirements

To avoid co-insurance penalties, property owners must ensure they carry insurance coverage equal to or above the co-insurance requirement. Regularly reviewing and updating insurance coverage can help avoid potential penalties and ensure adequate protection in the event of a partial loss.

Understanding co-insurance and its implications is essential for property owners seeking comprehensive insurance coverage and fair claim settlements. Always consult with an experienced insurance professional to assess your specific insurance needs and ensure you meet co-insurance requirements appropriately.

Top Reference Websites for Landlords: Your Essential Toolkit

As a landlord, having access to reliable and up-to-date resources is crucial for effectively managing rental properties, understanding legal obligations, and staying informed about industry trends. Whether you are a seasoned landlord or just starting your property management journey, these reference websites can serve as your essential toolkit:

1. Landlordology (www.landlordology.com):
   Landlordology is a comprehensive resource hub offering a wealth of articles, guides, and tools for landlords. From tenant screening tips to lease agreement templates, this website covers a wide range of topics to help landlords navigate various challenges and make informed decisions.

2. NOLO (www.nolo.com):
   NOLO is a trusted legal resource for landlords. It provides valuable insights into landlord-tenant law, rental property management, and legal forms. Landlords can access articles, books, and self-help legal guides to understand their rights and responsibilities in various situations.

3. The Balance Small Business (www.thebalancesmb.com):
   The Balance Small Business has a dedicated section for landlords, offering practical advice on managing rental properties, tenant relations, and property maintenance. It also covers financial aspects such as budgeting and taxation for rental income.

4. BiggerPockets (www.biggerpockets.com):
 BiggerPockets is a popular real estate investing community with a vast forum of landlords and property investors sharing insights and experiences. It offers articles, podcasts, and educational resources to help landlords grow their portfolio and make informed investment decisions.

5. Rental Housing Journal (www.rentalhousingjournal.com):
   Rental Housing Journal provides industry news, trends, and updates relevant to landlords and property managers. Stay informed about market changes, legislative updates, and

emerging best practices to enhance your rental property business.

6. National Apartment Association (www.naahq.org):
   The National Apartment Association is a leading advocate for the rental housing industry. Their website offers resources, research, and events to keep landlords abreast of industry developments and legislative matters.

7. Zillow Rental Manager (www.zillow.com/rental-manager):
   Zillow Rental Manager is a valuable online tool for landlords to advertise rental listings, screen potential tenants, and manage leases digitally. It streamlines the rental process and ensures efficient property management.

8. HUD.gov - Landlord Resources (www.hud.gov/program_offices/fair_housing_equal_opp/landlord):
   The U.S. Department of Housing and Urban Development (HUD) provides landlord resources, fair housing guidelines, and tools to promote compliance with federal housing regulations.

9. American Apartment Owners Association (www.american-apartment-owners-association.org):
   The American Apartment Owners Association offers educational resources, legal forms, and property management tools for landlords. It also provides access to insurance and tenant screening services.

10. TenantCloud (www.tenantcloud.com):
   TenantCloud is a property management software that helps landlords organize and streamline their rental business. It offers features like online rent collection, maintenance tracking, and tenant communication tools.

Utilize these reference websites to stay informed, make informed decisions, and enhance your effectiveness as a landlord. Remember that each website provides valuable information, but it's essential to cross-reference and seek professional advice when necessary. With the right resources at your disposal, you can confidently manage your rental properties and build a successful and thriving rental business.